D1161424

GRANDMA'S
Thanksgiving Dinner

Maria Hoskins
ILLUSTRATED BY PAIGE MASON

C&V 4 Seasons Publishing Company, LLC
Arkansas 2015

Acknowledgements

Special thanks to Paige Mason for bringing to life precious memories in the illustrations created for my book *Grandma's Thanksgiving Dinner*. In addition, many special thanks to Garbo Hearne, owner of Pyramid Art, Books, and Custom Framing, and her staff; Janis Kearney, author of the Best-Selling book *Cotton Field of Dreams;* and Patrick Oliver, literary consultant and author of *Turn the Page and Don't Stop,* for their guidance and support in the development of this children's book project. Also, I would like to thank my webpage designer Julian White; book designer Denise Billups, Editor Elisha Neubauer, for editing all of my project documents; and my church family and community for their support. Most of all, I would like to thank my family who provided guidance, discipline and encouragement. Your support and direction is very much appreciated!

Foreword

JANIS F. KEARNEY

Maria Hoskins is a storyteller and educator whose books offer young readers a bird's-eye view of rural farm life. More than just delightful storytelling, Hoskins takes great care to ensure that her beautiful illustrations result in a meaningful and enjoyable relationship for children. Author of the 2014 *Christmas Night on the Farm,* Maria Hoskins has once again brought her magical childhood memories of holidays on the farm to young readers in her new book, *Grandma's Thanksgiving Dinner.* Here, Hoskins shares memories of crisp autumn days on an Arkansas farm populated by a loving family and farm animals. Thanks to Hoskins' vivid memories, young readers will surely imagine waking up on Thanksgiving morning on the rural farm, feeling the warmth of the potbellied stove, and hearing the unique sounds from the barn that can only be heard on a farm.

Grandma's Thanksgiving Dinner is a special treat for children with no experience of farm life. They will be drawn into a world filled with love, doting parents, guardians and community members, and lively farm animals. Hoskins aptly shares a brief history lesson with her young readers about rural America and the age-old traditions of farm living.

Finally, Hoskins' story will surely entice the most reticent of readers as they imagine the tastes, the textures, the smells of the sweet potato pie, turkey and dressing, ham and homemade rolls! A most delightful potpourri of life on the farm on Thanksgiving Day.

3

4

Today we are going to Grandma's house for Thanksgiving Dinner. My sister, my brother, and I love to eat Grandma's farm-grown, home cooked food!

Grandma lives on a small farm with my uncle and aunt. On the farm, there are lots of animals: horses, cows, pigs, chickens, a mule, and a little Beagle named Boy. In the front yard is a big tree with a monkey swing, just for me.

8

It is a cool, fall day; the sky is blue, and leaves cover the ground like a colorful blanket. Grandma's house has a potbelly stove and as the smoke comes out of the chimney, it looks like cotton balls floating into the sky.

In the kitchen is a big dinner table, set properly with Grandma's finest china. On the left side of each plate is a knife and spoon; a dinner fork and a salad fork sit on the right side, and a dessert fork lies across the top. A water glass, tea glass, and fabric napkin are also set at everyplace. Grandma is a hard worker but is very serious about table etiquette, so no one is allowed to sit at the table until dinner is served.

There is so much to eat! There is turkey with dressing, ham, yams, pinto beans, chitterlings, potato salad, greens, macaroni and cheese, and homemade rolls!

Mmm... It looks delicious. The sweet smell of the desserts that Grandma and Momma have made smells so good! They have every kind of pie you could want: sweet potato pie, egg custard pie, pecan pie, peach cobbler, and apple-pie! Yum!

Just before it's time to eat, family and friends arrive. Aunts, uncles, cousins, and family friends – even our church pastor stops by to eat some of Grandma's delicious meal.

The food is set out on the dinner table and every-one gather around the old potbelly stove, hold-ing hands, as Uncle Odus says a prayer of thanks for our many blessings.

15

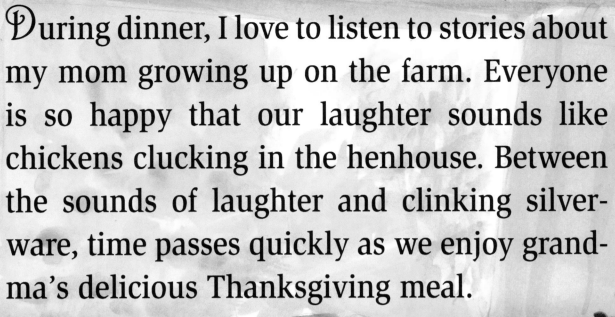

During dinner, I love to listen to stories about my mom growing up on the farm. Everyone is so happy that our laughter sounds like chickens clucking in the henhouse. Between the sounds of laughter and clinking silverware, time passes quickly as we enjoy grandma's delicious Thanksgiving meal.

18

Dinner is over,
everyone is full,
and no one wants
to move.

19

But it's time to clear off the table, and clean the kitchen, while Grandma boxes meals for those who may be elderly, sick, or who just may need a meal.

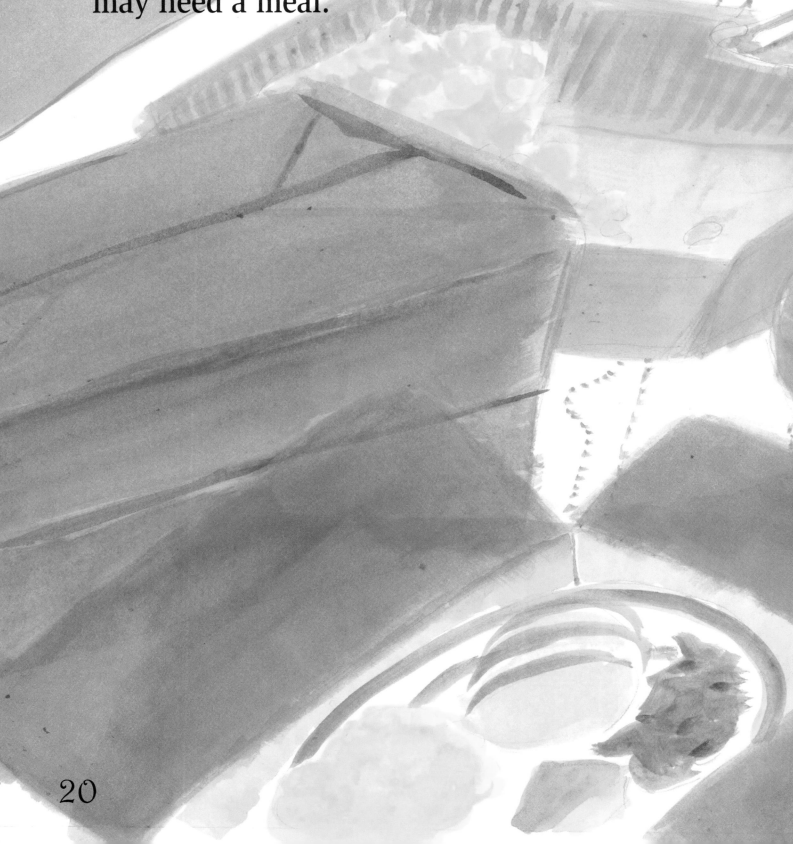

Oh, how much fun we had at Grandma's Thanksgiving dinner! I can't wait until we come back to Grandma's house for Christmas Night on the Farm.

What did your family do for Thanksgiving?
Write your Thanksgiving story:

Add your Thanksgiving story
illustrations or photos:

This book is dedicated to the memory of my Grandma Lillie Ella Collins, Uncle W.O. Collins, Aunt Vernice Collins, sister Jeannie Ryan, children of Lillie and Sam Collins, and the many elders of the Palarm Community who bonded together to help one another and have passed away. I also dedicate this book to my husband, Archie Hoskins, who I dearly love. He is my partner, my friend; that consistent voice in my life that helps me to stay on task as we work together, pray together, care for our family and live our lives together. To my wonderful children, Christina and Victoria – two precious blessings from God! I am blessed to be their mother. To my brother Freddy, I am so thankful that we are very close and for the memories with both my brother and sister; to Papa Alvin Gill, with love and appreciation for everything he does to support our family; and to my Mom, Berthenia L. Gill – the rock of this family. Thank you for being the wonderful person you are, grooming and teaching your children to stay faithful and do good; always giving, even when you did not have it to give, and setting the example not only for your children, but for children and adults wherever you go. Thank you for so many wonderful memories and great times spent on the Collins Farm in Mayflower, Arkansas.

Childhood memories stay with us all of our lives. As parents, aunts, uncles, sisters, brothers, or caregivers, it is up to us to instill good memories in the minds of those we care for. I pray that my children, Christina and Victoria, will forever recall heartfelt stories based on love that will bring smiles to their faces and joy to their hearts.

As the author of this book, I pray this story will give readers a glimpse of how a strong and loving family can create lifetime memories, by eating a meal with family and friends during a visit to Grandma's house on Thanksgiving.

Happy Thanksgiving!

CPSIA information can be obtained at www.ICGtesting.com
Printed in the USA
BVIW12n0641020617
485817BV00002B/6